Sea Lions

Victoria Blakemore

Copyright info/picture credits

Cover, SE Viera Photo/AdobeStock; Page 3, gkgegk/Pixabay; Page 5, Barni1/Pixabay; Page 7, Alexas_Fotos/Pixabay; Page 9, dimitrivetsikas1969/Pixabay; Pages 10-11, Ayrat A./AdobeStock; Page 13, Glenn/AdobeStock; Page 15, Ashton/AdobeStock; Page 17, sebastian_photos/Pixabay; Page 19, David Litman/Shutterstock; Page 21, Gellinger/Pixabay; Page 23; skeeze/Pixabay; Page 25, wim claes/Shutterstock; Page 27, SoleneC1/Pixabay; Page 29, 2204574/Pixabay; Page 31, Pexels/Pixabay; Page 33, SE Viera Photo/AdobeStock

Table of Contents

What Are Sea Lions?

Sea lions are a special kind of mammal called a **pinniped**. This means that they have flippers instead of feet. Other **pinnipeds** include seals and walruses.

There are six different kinds of sea lions. They differ in size, color, and where they live.

Sea lions can be a mix of brown, black, yellow, and white in color.

Size

Sea lions can grow to be between four and about eleven feet long. When fully grown, they can range from about 100 to over 2,000 pounds in weight.

Different kinds of sea lions grow to be different sizes. The largest kind of sea lion is the steller sea lion.

Male sea lions are usually
much larger than female sea
lions.

5

Physical Characteristics

Sea lions have a thick layer of fat that is called **blubber**. It helps to keep them warm when they are in icy waters.

They also have a short coat of fur. Sea lions **molt** once each year. When they **molt**, they shed their old fur and grow new fur.

Sea lions have long whiskers. Their whiskers are called **vibrissae**. They help sea lions to sense movement around in the water.

Habitat

Sea lions are found around the coast. They spend time on land and in the ocean, so they need to be close to shore. Some live in warm areas, others live where it is cold.

They are often seen along rocky coasts. They also spend time on piers, docks, and **buoys**.

Range

Sea lions are found in and around the Pacific ocean.

They are seen along the coasts of places like the United States, Australia, and New Zealand.

11

Diet

Sea lions are **carnivores**. They eat only meat. They do not need to drink water. They get the water they need from the food they eat.

Their diet is made up of fish, squid, crabs, and clams. Larger sea lions, such as the steller sea lion, also eat seals.

Sea lions have sharp teeth, but they usually swallow their food whole.

Sea lions use their whiskers, or **vibrissae** to help them find food. The whiskers move in the water and help to sense movement.

Some sea lions spend over fifteen hours each day diving for food. They can dive over one hundred times to catch enough prey to eat.

Sea lions can dive up to 600 feet below the surface of the water.

They can stay underwater for about twenty minutes.

Communication

Sea lions use mainly sound and movement to communicate. Certain body **postures** can be used to send messages.

Sea lions are very **vocal** animals. They make many different sounds. They are able to make sounds on land and underwater.

Sea lions can bark, whistle, click, moan, chirp, growl, and squeak. Mothers and pups also have special sounds that they use to find one another.

Movement

Sea lions have been known to swim up to about twenty miles per hour. They sometimes leap out of the water as they swim. This is called porpoising. It helps them to swim faster.

When on land, sea lions use their flippers and tail to move around. They are much slower on land.

Sea lions are often seen floating in the water with their flippers in the air. This is called rafting. It helps them to cool off if they are hot.

Sea Lion Pups

Sea lions usually have one baby, or pup. They are born with a thick coat of fur that keeps them warm. The mothers feed their pups milk. The milk helps the pups to grow their layer of **blubber**.

Pups are able to walk shortly after they are born. They learn to swim within a few weeks.

Sea lion pups spend about a year with their mother. The mother teaches her pups how to hunt and survive. 21

Sea Lion Life

Sea lions are very social animals. They live in large groups that are called colonies. When the groups are made up of mothers and pups, they are called rookeries.

Sea lions spend most of their time resting on land or diving underwater for food.

Sea lions are often seen resting

together in groups on land.

Sometimes they sleep on top of

each other.

23

Sea Lion or Seal?

Sea lions and seals are very similar. They can be hard to tell apart. However, there are a few key differences.

Sea lions are able to rotate their **hind** flippers. This allows them to move on land. Seals cannot rotate their flippers. It is harder for them to move on land.

Sea lions have special ear flaps on their head. Seals only have small holes for their ears.

Population

Of the six kinds of sea lions, two are **endangered**. Their populations are **declining** in the wild. They could become **extinct**.

The Japanese sea lion is already **extinct**. There are no more left in the wild.

Sea lions usually live up to twenty years. Some have lived as long as thirty years. Females usually live longer than males.

Sea Lions in Danger

Sea lions are facing many threats in the wild. Many **parasites** and diseases can make sea lions sick. Pollution in the ocean and on land can also hurt sea lions.

In some places, sea lion habitats are being destroyed for buildings and **commercial** fishing.

Sea lions can also get caught on fishing lines and in nets. When they get caught, they can't get to the surface to breathe.

Helping Sea Lions

In some places, sea lions are protected by laws. The laws are there to keep them safe from being hunted.

Some people **volunteer** their time to help sea lions that are **stranded**. They try to figure out what made the sea lions sick and how they can help them.

Some groups are working to help sea lions that are sick or hurt. They take care of them until they can be released back into the wild.

Other groups focus on research. They want to learn more about sea lions so they can find more ways to help them.

Glossary

Blubber: a thick layer of fat

Buoy: a float attached by line to the bottom of a body of water to mark a place

Carnivore: an animal that eats only meat

Commercial: having to do with trade or business

Declining: getting smaller

Endangered: at risk of becoming extinct

Extinct: when there are no more of an animal left in the wild

Hind: back

Molt: to shed old fur and grow new fur

Parasite: a plant or animal that feeds on the energy of another animal

Pinniped: a mammal that has flippers instead of feet

Posture: the position of a body

Stranded: when an animal that is sick or hurt is stuck on the shore

Vibrissae: whiskers that help to sense movement

Vocal: making lots of noises

Volunteer: when someone offers to work or help without pay

About the Author

Victoria Blakemore is a first grade

teacher in Southwest Florida with a

passion for reading.

You can visit her at

www.elementaryexplorers.com

Also in This Series

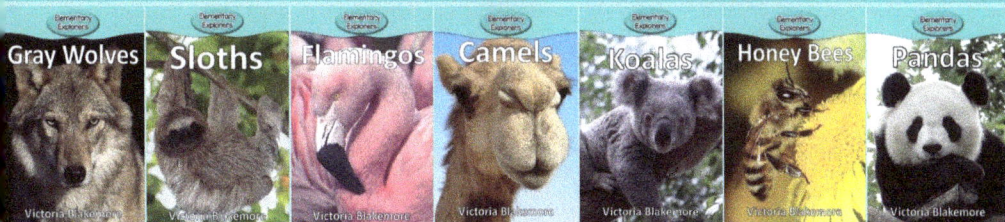

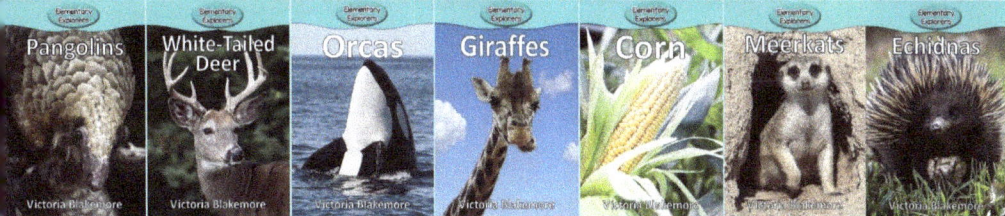

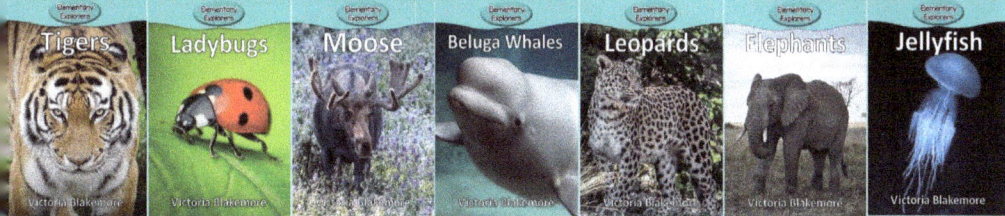

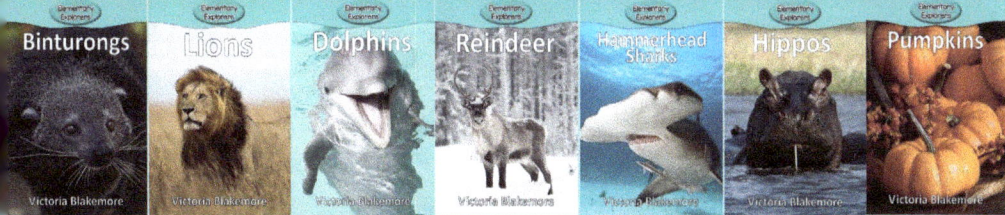

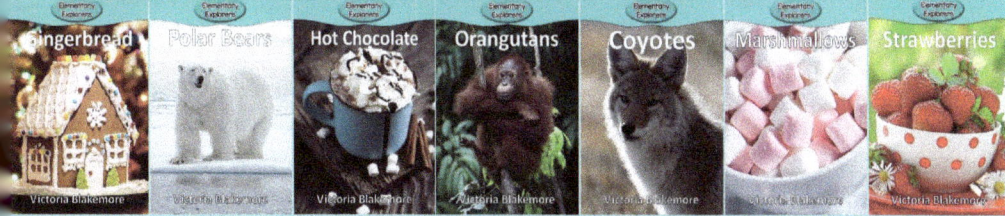

Gray Wolves	Sloths	Flamingos	Camels	Koalas	Honey Bees	Pandas
Pangolins	White-Tailed Deer	Orcas	Giraffes	Corn	Meerkats	Echidnas
Walruses	Raccoons	Bald Eagles	Apples	Arctic Foxes	Red Pandas	Cassowaries
Tigers	Ladybugs	Moose	Beluga Whales	Leopards	Elephants	Jellyfish
Binturongs	Lions	Dolphins	Reindeer	Hammerhead Sharks	Hippos	Pumpkins
Peafowl	Chameleons	Florida Panthers	Aye-Ayes	Black Bears	Cheetahs	Manatees
Gingerbread	Polar Bears	Hot Chocolate	Orangutans	Coyotes	Marshmallows	Strawberries

Victoria Blakemore

Also in This Series

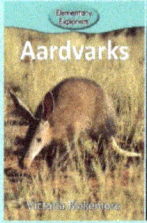

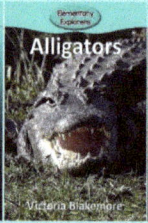

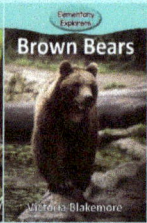

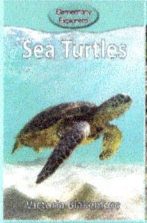

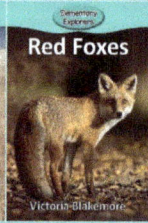

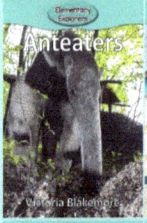

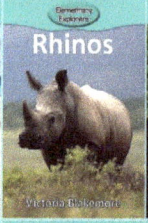

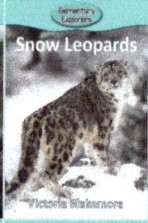

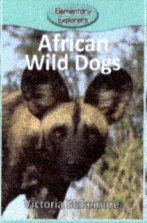

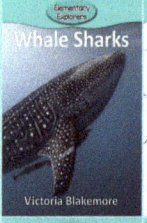

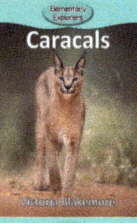

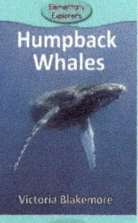

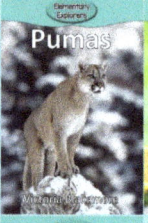

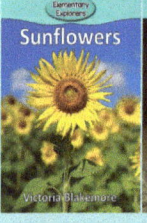

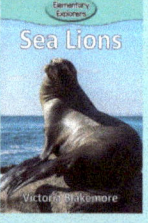

Aardvarks	Mako Sharks	Alligators	Frogs	Hedgehogs	Brown Bears	Bongos
Sea Turtles	Quokkas	Muskrats	Zebras	Red Foxes	Ring-Tailed Lemurs	Platypuses
Anteaters	Kangaroos	Rhinos	Jaguars	Wombats	Capybaras	Gorillas
Cats	Skunks	Butterflies	Dingoes	Snow Leopards	African Wild Dogs	Penguins
Whale Sharks	Wolverines	Warthogs	Caracals	Badgers	Seals	Hummingbirds
Pikas	Humpback Whales	Pumas	Lemonade	Llamas	Tulips	Ostriches
Sunflowers	Fennec Foxes	Sea Lions				

Victoria Blakemore

www.ingramcontent.com/pod-product-compliance
Lightning Source LLC
Chambersburg PA
CBHW051253020426
42333CB00025B/3195